MY HEART WEARS NO COLORS

¤

Nancy Owen Nelson

FUTURECYCLE PRESS

www.futurecycle.org

Cover image from page 161 of Frank Leslie's Scenes and Portraits of the Civil War (1894); photo of Confederate soldier (renactment) by Danny Rebb Fine Art Photography; back cover author photo by Joy Gaines-Friedler; photo of the author at the tombstone of N. J. Owen by Roger Zeigler; photo of Charley Owen courtesy of Karen Grubaugh; Chandler plot photo donated by Beth Presley; Owen Family Reunion ca 1896 photo by Carole Kane; cover and interior book design by Diane Kistner; Avenir Next text, Avenir Condensed and Ruslan Display titling

Published by FutureCycle Press
Athens, Georgia, USA

ISBN 978-1-942371-65-6

For my father, son of the South,
with a heart of justice

Contents

Charlottesville...9

A Family Name..10

William Joseph Owen Applies for
    Needy Confederate Soldiers Relief, 1896................12

Charley A. Owen...14

War Between the States..16

My Civil War..17

I Am Folding My Flag...19

Minzie Mary Russell Talks on the 11th Regiment,
    Tennessee Cavalry..21

Vigil Strange: After Walt Whitman...................................22

Nannie B. Russell...24

Mary Russell Humphrey...26

Ghosts: Francis Marion Chandler.....................................27

Found on Ancestry.com: Fifteen Slaves...........................30

Stayin' On..32

Afterword, Notes...34

My subject is War, and the pity of War.
The Poetry is in the pity.

—Wilfred Owen

Charlottesville

August 11-12, 2017

Torches lit by hate on a bucolic campus,
night-marchers to reverse the course of
your shameful history. In the shadow of
the man who could have gone to either
side, blue or gray, who made the ill-fated choice
for region, not country, you do the same,
hatemongers. You turn us backward, not
forward. You hinder the birth of a new home
where principles you espouse of liberty,
freedom, belong to all who breathe,
who have life on this land.

You shame those who went before you,
who crawled out of a bloody history
to make a life of peace.

Step aside.

Allow those who share your blood,
your land, your country,
allow us go forward without you.

A Family Name

Her trunk smells of another time
one hundred years ago.
Civil War.

Locks stick. I force them open,
break a fingernail. Rust clings
to metal spotted with old paint
and varnish, once shining golden,
like brass.

Big with child, I dust inside,
pull yellowed paper lining, thin
as onion skin, tossed aside easy,
like a breath.

Next, cloth to line it, calico print—
red, white, black—not the colors
of Confederacy or Union. I staple,
glue cloth to rounded top, flattened
sides. Wait for it to dry.
I clean the outer surface, rigid,
 uneven from time and wear.

Her fingers touched, pulled, packed
dresses, hats, baby shoes, maybe
even Grandmama Steve's booties, knit from
soft pink thread, ribbon woven
through to tie her feet, tiny toes still
curled from lying inside her mother.

Time to paint. I choose black,
a shiny paint to smooth
roughened sides, bring metal
locks forward for the eye,

seal wooden bands, bowed over
top, soft now like sanded wood.

I never knew her, Nancy Owen.
She never knew me, nor the son
I would bear, named for her.

I sit up straight to view my labor,
My back aches and my legs stiffen.
Straining to stand, I carry her namesake
tucked inside me. Soon, my fingers will
raise the latch, fold his tiny clothes into
the rich calico lining, colors not of war,
but colors of peace.

The author at the grave of her great grandmother and namesake,
Nancy Jane Thomason Owen

William Joseph Owen Applies for Needy Confederate Soldiers Relief, 1896

"I was at Shiloh, at Hattiesburg.
I fought the enemy of your country,
survived to fight again, even when men
and horses in your unit marched and walked
more than 1200 miles weary, thirsty,
hungry, hooves and pantlegs collecting dust."

When he was sixty-six, he applied
for financial relief. "Rheumatism and
general disability," he wrote.

What he did not write was how it was at Shiloh,
how he hated to leave his wife and five kids
and go to war, how he was 'scripted.

"I dodged and ducked during
artillery fires from flaming muskets,
grasses and trees and friends burning around me.
We thought we had surprised the Billy Yanks,
but not so.
Instead, we watched our brothers gag,
bleed out, at Hornet's Nest. And how,
exhausted, the Rebs crawled
and sneaked up and over hill after hill until,
fearing the worst, we heard of General
Johnston's death, shot in the leg. And how,
though we thought there would be a lull,
the hellish battle continued, and more Yanks
came with General Grant. And how,
even with Wallace's troops, we,
the still living, had to retreat."

He went on to fight other battles.

***

But in his application for relief he
wrote only what he owned:

Personal Property Value
1 horses and mules $50.00

In the regiment, they said he was
 a "great horse trader."
Heard tell he and his brother Charley
stole horses and cattle from the Yanks.

Cattle of all kinds
Hogs, sheep, & goats
Mechanical and farming tools and implements

He was listed as "farmer,
head of the house"
after the war, in 1870 and 1880 censuses.

Pistols, guns,
1 watches, clocks and jewelry $10.00
Household and kitchen furniture $15.00
1 bicycles and vehicles $40.00
Goods, wares and merchandise
Total $115.00

So little property, so long a life.

Charley A. Owen

Winston County, Alabama, 1867

How I ended up here, I'll never know. Came to see
my friend William's widow, Martha Jane, took a fancy to her.
Both of them Cupp boys, William
and Hugh, fought with me and my brother Bill
in the 7th Alabama unit. Bill and me survived Shiloh,
but the Cupps didn't come home.

But how did I end up in this Union county that
never joined the rebels? How can I stay here after
I married William Cupp's bride, stayed here with her,
with John and Mary, their boy and girl?
Why, John was just a young thing, four months old,
when his daddy died. I loved his mama when I first
laid eyes on her, loved her so much I couldn't wait
to have her, kids and all. Loved them both, 'cause
they were hers. And his.

How can I stay in the county where men
at Looney's Tavern refused to sign the oath to
our rebel cause? Here I am now, a farmer with
wife and three kids. Can't even vote. A great horse
trader, Bill and me stole from the Yanks, stole
cattle for food, horses for our men who marched
1200 miles in five months. Plum wore out we were.
So yeh, we stole them horses and we stole them cattle.
We had to eat. We had to move.
We just had to.

But here I am in this Union county, outcast, branded as a rebel.
This is my state too, Consarnit!
Can't wait for everything to be right again.
Can't wait to start my new life with Martha Jane.

Can't wait to start our farm
on this land, where Bill and me was raised.

Cullman County, Alabama, 1910

You made it alright, Charley. Family stories
have it that your friend William Cupp died
in your arms, early in the war, in Virginia.
That you rode home to Morgan County at war's end,
triumphant on a white horse. That you rode
that same horse to Township 12, Winston County,
to comfort his widow. That when you told her
about her husband, she fell into your arms. And
that was the beginning of love.

You became a man of the Lord, a preacher,
intent on saving souls. Were you tempted to
cast damnation on those in Winston County who
denied you the vote?

I don't think so. You were too busy farming,
raising eleven children, with Martha Jane's two,
saving souls, collecting taxes, until in your
later years the wear of war and work caught
up to you and, diabetic, you slowed down,
got ready to die.

You were a good man, Charley Owen. A man who
loved his friend, loved his wife, his god and, I'm sure,
even after this divisive war,
his country.

Charley Owen

War Between the States

Prescott, Arizona, 2010

A man in Apple Pan Restaurant
orders breakfast. Scrambled eggs,
biscuit, bacon—crisp—and coffee.
His shirt displays "Civil War"
at the top, his midsection covered
with a map of the South—
West Virginia, Virginia, Carolinas
spread across his belly, rebel flag
on his right shoulder.
He's armed, "packin' heat," as they say
here in Arizona. Saving himself from a
terrorist government that gives
Socialist welfare to poor, underserving,
lazy people.

It's a rough world out there. His reading specs
perched on the end of his nose,
he holds a book over his coffee and eggs:
The Gift of Fear—Survival Signals
That Protect Us from Violence.
This book must give him safety, a sense
of protection.

Maybe he's not crazy after all. Maybe
the fear I had of him when I saw his shirt,
his shorn hair, his gun, is only as real
as his fear—the kind that makes him
wear a shirt remembering a country
torn apart by blood of families, torn
by people fearing things that would
never happen.

Maybe he won't even have to use that gun.

My Civil War

You may not tell me what color my heart wears,
gray or blue. You may not tell me what color
I bleed when I think of the anguish of brother
against brother, cousin against cousin,
crops burned in the fields so babies could
not eat, men returning home without an arm,
a leg.

When Johnny comes marching home again
he may find his home in the land of cotton
is gone. His house may be burned to the ground,
his children and wife sent into woods. Or maybe
he won't come marching home because he is
in prison, or maybe he won't come marching home
at all.

There were resisters who hid runaway slaves
in churches, in the woods of North Alabama;
there was the Free State of Winston County,
Alabama, which seceded from this wrong cause—
Free State of Jones, Mississippi, where men,
black and white, fought together; where they
went to the polls to vote Republican, the
party of Lincoln; where some of the blacks
ended up dead, like Johnny, but worse—hung,
trussed to a tree like
so much meat.

There was Robert E. Lee, who told Lincoln
"No thank you," when asked to lead the Union.
Instead, he made the tragic choice to
to serve his statesmen, and not the nation he loved.

There were those both blue and gray
who mourned when Abe went down,

who knew, even in defeat, the gaping hole
he left behind.

I think I would have joined the Free State
of Winston, Alabama.
I think I would have taken a wagon north
to Madison County, knocked on the door
of my kin, and begged them not to fight
for this cause that divided brother
from brother, cousin from cousin.

But there were those long Alabama
summer afternoons when, after a sandwich
of meatloaf, bread, and catsup in Big Mama's
kitchen, a glass of sweet iced tea, potato
salad and stuffed eggs, I'd nap
in her back bedroom under a ceiling fan,
waves of warm air lifting above and away
from me. I'd hear in the distance the faint voice
of Aunt Mandy in the kitchen, singing a hymn
softly under her breath while she washed dishes
in hot, steaming bubbly water. And there were
the late afternoons on Sunday at Papa
and Mama Steve's house, aunts, and uncles and
Cousin Ann sitting on the porch, just talking, just
laughing, until the sun set and fireflies came
out. Even after dark, the talk and laughter went on
while Ann and I captured lightning bugs,
little flying fires, in a glass jar, only to let them
go before their fluttering lights ceased.

So, still, you may not tell me the color my heart
wears or what color I bleed. My heart wears
no color, except that of peace. I bleed for history,
for lives lost in a cause that still divides us.

I Am Folding My Flag

It whips in the wind,
carries a sharp, stinging
message, insistent on
obedience.
Adorns car windows,
walls of Walmart and
freezers in the grocery,
back windows of pickup
trucks with *Proud to be
American* bumper stickers.

Frozen in time, men
struggle to raise it in
the midst of battle,
statues of liberty they
become, monuments
to justice and freedoms
now lost in transition to
another, harsher world.

Little men in a coffee shop
laugh and read the paper.
They try to straighten
their old backs as they
praise aggression and power,
not the red of blood spilled
for freedom, the blue
of a prairie sky at dawn,
or the white of a banner
of peace.

I was born on Flag Day.
As a child, I thought the
flags flew for me. June
14, a day of celebration.

I watched soldiers salute
it, heard the anthem,
felt the vibrating notes
in my chest, pride
of a nation I thought was
fair and good. When Daddy
died, I watched as the men
lay down their rifles, folded
the flag atop his coffin, folded it
into a tight triangle of cloth
to keep the memory of a life
lived for peace.

I cannot write this poem.

Yes, the flag that draped my father's
coffin on a rainy March afternoon
was folded, and folded again and
again, until it formed a triangle
of loss, a heavy burden for Mother.

I cannot write this poem.

Instead, I am folding my flag,
its stars and stripes, its reds whites
blues. These colors *do* run.
They run everywhere, onto
shirts and cars and store
fronts, restaurant windows,
cash registers. They run
into the hands and faces,
the hearts and minds of the angry,
the righteous.

I cannot write this poem.

I am folding my flag.

Minzie Mary Russell Talks on the
11th Regiment, Tennessee Cavalry

August 1, 1863

I didn't want them to go. Told my man Archie,
"My boys don't b'long with that Tennessee outfit,
where they don't take good care of them 'Bama boys."
Did he hear me? No indeed. Never does listen.
All he cares about is this rebellion, the pride of region,
state, farmland where them rich folks' slaves work,
sweat out their hearts over cotton, bend and stoop,
gasp in the bald heat of cotton-picking summer.

All any of 'em care about is this gall-dang war,
men shootin' at other men, some of 'em young enough
to be in school. Why, I even had plans for Calvin,
my youngest, my baby. Wanted him to go to East Alabama
Male College, learn Latin, maybe Greek, make something
of himself b'sides just being a farmer. Maybe be a lawyer,
like Abe Lincoln. Not telling Archie that part, for sure.
He'd probably never let me back in the house.

Don't matter no way, now that Calvin's gone,
dead months ago, end of March—24th, to be exact.
Buried in the Russell plot where I'll be laid to rest
someday not too far from now. Joined the war
only one month after the Tennessee came together
with some other companies. It was only one month
before my Calvin died.

I'm weary, tired to the bone after birthing eight babies,
after raisin' them to work hard, plow and cut,
bake and clean. What's the point anymore, when
my baby boy, my favorite, is dead.
All because of this stupid war.
Tired, weary to the bone.

Vigil Strange: After Walt Whitman

John R. Russell
March 27, 1863

My little brother, I stood over you—ill,
on a pallet, rebel uniform torn, smudged with blood,
shit mud. In the morning, you couldn't even drink
the coffee we boiled in camp, after we brushed off the
maggots from 'top of the beans. You couldn't eat
the sloosh we fixed—cornmeal and bacon grease,
nothing like the cornbread and greens Mama fixed
for us. We had to do with what we had.

When I heard that rebel yell in Brentwood,
the morning after you died, I didn't want to
fight, didn't want to go against Col. Bloodgood.
I didn't care whether we called a truce or whether
he surrendered. My baby brother was gone.
All I could do was stand with my musket, wait
for the cannon balls to blast, splitting my ear
drums, while horses bellowed. I could only walk
forward toward the line of Billy Yanks
like the dead man I already was.

Afterward, after we won that battle, I stepped
over the piles of bodies, Yankees mostly, and
trudged back to camp to find you, shrouded
and lying on the ground. I buried you in a
shallow grave, one of our fellows playing
"Dixie" on his harmonica. Only a few stood by.
I read from the Bible, Ecclesiastes, *time to be born,
and a time to die; a time to plant.* But mumbled
the rest about killing under my breath,
not believing it was yet *a time to heal.*

I remembered those verses from Bethel Church
where we'd sing our hymns without instruments,
where our elders or deacons would read from
the text, sometimes these same words I read over your
young body. Those words didn't make any sense to me
when I heard 'em before. When I read 'em over you,
I didn't want to believe there is a time to die.
I still don't. At least not the time for you to die now.

Speaking of believin', I think about all that singing,
all those words about peace and love we heard at
church. I think about how and why we're fighting
this war. Why, when our family doesn't even
own slaves! Never have, never will, is my pledge.

I'll take you home, young brother Calvin, take
you home slung over my horse, the one I
brought from the farm when we left to follow
Holman, before we had to join General Wheeler
because we couldn't be partisan rangers any more,
on our own. Maybe if we'd stayed independent,
maybe, just maybe, you wouldn't be dead.

When I take you home, Calvin, walking my horse
up mountains and down into the green valleys,
I will pass by the rail line from Nashville to
Decatur. If there's a train coming through,
I'll stop and wait, raise my hat in the air,
listen to the lone sound of the whistle
bringing you back to Mama.

Nannie B. Russell

July 25, 1904

Mama had me in July, my special month.
Youngest of four sisters, Mary, Vina,
and Sallie. After we all came along,
Papa and Mama never stopped
hoping for a boy. They had one, born
on a summer day like the rest of us.
Born dead he was. In August.
Not in July.

Hope I never lose a baby.

July is indeed a blessed month for me.
Tomorrow I marry Robert, a tall,
beautiful man I met at the Bethel Church.
Tomorrow I'll wear my white dress
with the pretty, pearl-like flower buttons.

One Sunday last winter, Robert came
for the first time, sat down in a back pew.
He was already there when we arrived.
When everybody stood up, went around
to shake hands, Robert rose up from the pew,
turned toward me to shake hands, and oh my,
was he tall! Towered over me. Had to crane
my neck to look at his face. All during the singing
he stared at me like he'd never heard
a woman sing so pretty.

So tomorrow, I marry this tall man, Robert.
He wants babies. He wants to open a store
in the big city of Decatur! I have butterflies
in my tummy thinking about my white
dress with those pretty flower buttons.

I love those buttons. They remind me of
Robert, of the flowers he picked for me
when we took a walk. They remind me
of the children we will have.

Tomorrow will be another reason
why I love the month of July.

July 13, 1905

This July was not kind to you, Nannie B.
You and Robert were happy for less than
one year. Yesterday, you birthed a baby girl
and died an hour after she emerged
from your body.

Your baby girl will live long, 96 years
to your 26. Her daughter will hold
those wedding buttons in her hand.
She will wind about them strands
of the baby girl's hair.

Mary Russell Humphrey

1908

So they took her away, my little Nannie B,
three years old. She knew only me. I was her
mother since she came out, bloody and screaming,
from my sister's womb. I fed her meal mush,
tried to make my breasts give forth milk.
My youngest, John, was six, and it had
been too long since he sucked my breasts.
There was nothing left.

But I gave her love, and she gave it back.
Then that day, confused and crying,
she reached out for me while her tall daddy
and his new wife took her away in a wagon,
away from me.

What do I do now? How do I go on without
my sister's baby girl with me? How do I see
the next day coming? I don't like my husband,
and he doesn't like me or his children. Spends
time in the barn sawing and pounding, never
comes inside except to eat and sleep. Snores
all night too. But when the little girl was with
me, I would go into her bed, hold her close,
pretend she was mine. Or I'd pretend her mother
did not die having her. That she was just on
a short little trip into town.

Ghosts: Francis Marion Chandler

1835-1899

I married Euphremia in '68,
we started our family. Five kids,
four boys and a girl. Ran a farm.
Did ok with my life.

Even so, every night I hear the screams
of my brothers.

I fought for the good cause against Grant
at Fort Donelson, saw us go down in dust,
surrender to the Yanks. We gave up the gateway
to the Confederacy, the Cumberland River,
on that day in February, 1862.

Made up for it in '64, at Big Shanty.
Sherman had control for two weeks,
June 10-24. But we overcame him,
went between two mountains, killed
more than 3000 Yanks.

Then there was Fort Deposit. I was so
proud to be in that fight! We couldn't
hold the Cumberland, but we held
the Tennessee River, the sole entry
to North Alabama ('cept by wagon
or horse). Felt like I did something
that day, 15th of November, 1864, helped
protect my home and family in Jackson.

We served with Jeff Davis' 4th Regiment,
Alabama Cavalry, Companies G and B.
I made it to corporal by the time I mustered

out in May, 1865. I would have stayed in,
fought for the cause, if Lee hadn't
surrendered to Grant at Appomattox.

I could have died then, could have been
buried here in Union Cemetery before
my time. I made it, and they didn't.

Do I hear the ghosts of my rebel
brothers crying out at night?
Indeed, I do. Just wish I could have
helped more of 'em. Wish I could
have stayed in the fight longer. Wish
we'd won the war.

But still, I ended up with $800 real estate,
$400 personal estate.

Glad I could
do that much for my family.

Chandler Plot,
Union Cemetery,
Woodville, Alabama

Owen Reunion ca 1896. The man sitting down with the Bible is Charley Owen.

Found on Ancestry.com: Fifteen Slaves

Only ages, no names,
from three to seventy years
says the 1850 census.

I see them now on a
farm in Limestone, Alabama.
An old black man walks
with a cane past his owner.

"Good morning ma'am." "Yes ma'am,"
he says, body bent from
decades of labor over balls
of white cotton, bright as sunshine.
Makes his eyes burn.

A three-year-old girl runs
circles around her mother,
her hair in skinny pigtails,
"Picaninny," the kids at the
big house call her.
She doesn't understand what
it means. Only knows
it's not a happy, pretty name.

Her mama's hair's tied
in bandana, blue and red,
colors of the flag
except for white, color of
cotton, color of her owner's skin.

Mama scrubs a floor. Sweat
soaks her bandana,
runs down her face and neck.

She's thirty. She's finished,
she thinks, *'cause what else*
can be ahead for me? A husband
in the fields, six chilluns, some
young and underfoot, two of 'em boys
almost men? Men who will have
their own women, they chilluns
but won't be free of the lash,
the chains?

***

My father's
father's
father's
father,
how could his blood run through
my veins? How can I, these many
years later, own this truth,
own this inheritance—
blistered by sun, worn by labor,
not free?

Stayin' On

1862, Near Selma, Alabama

George Chambers, six years old, drives cows
and calves, tans leather, shucks corn for
the "Massa." He wears shoes with nails and tacks,
is up before sunrise, plays marbles with other
kids. Watches while the grownups make
ashcake on open coals in the fireplace—mix
of cornmeal and water, bubbling on the coals,
flipped, turned over 'til done.

When the war starts, he hears the big guns
all the way from Columbus. "De Yankees
come.... I was on de swamp wid 'leven head
of horses and some of Mistress' fine things
from de house. Us worked two or three years
'fore dey told us we was free."

March 7 1965, "Bloody Sunday," Selma, Alabama

They just want the right to vote. They march
arm-in-arm with Martin, including Jimmie Lee.
The troopers beat Jimmie, shoot him in the belly,
just 'cause he defends his grandfather and
mother from the beatings. He will die eight
days later. But, nonetheless, marchers cross
Edmund Pettus Bridge. They do not give up.
They march all the way to Montgomery.
They shall overcome.

July 23, 1967, Detroit, Michigan

Streets are alight with flame. Cars burned, windows
broken. White people flee the city. Like George
Chambers, they carry *their* fine things into the suburbs.

1400 buildings burned, over 7000 people arrested,
43 people dead. The next year Martin will say,
"American has failed to hear that the
promises of freedom and justice have not been met."
Whites care more about "tranquility and the status quo
than about justice and humanity."

July 23, 2017, Detroit, Michigan

The city is 80% black. Mr. Jones won't forget National
Guard tanks rolling down his street. At eight, he was a
delivery boy for fish and poultry. As he ducked glass bottles,
he heard raucous yells: "Nigger, get out of my neighborhood!"
Yet his family stayed in their beloved city.
In 2012, Mr. Jones lost his house to foreclosure.

October 7, 1937, Near Selma, Alabama

George Chambers speaks: "Us worked two or three years
'fore dey told us we was free. Den dey giv' us a little money
or so much crop and us stayed on."

Mr. Jones stayed on.
The marchers stayed on.
George Chambers stayed on.

In 1937, George says,
"De little [chilluns] all had big times. Dey played marbles,"
and, "Almost home so dey say, so dey say."

¤

Afterword

When I began researching the mystery surrounding my grand-mother, Nannie B. Russell Chandler, I did not know what I would find in my ancestral history. Though I was aware that my ancestors lived during the Civil War in the South, primarily in Alabama, I was unprepared for the impact of this knowledge on my understanding of myself and my history.

After publication of my memoir, *Searching for Nannie B: Connecting Three Generations of Southern Women* (Ardent Writers Press, 2015), I began to think about these ancestors, many of whom had Confederate States Army stones which were engraved with the specific companies and infantries in which these men served. I asked myself, how can I belong to the same blood line as these people who came before me? What, if anything, can or should I do to understand them? To disclaim the legacy of slavery they seemed to represent?

These questions resulted not only in soul searching but also in research into the Civil War, the culture and values of the South, and the lives of these ancestors as I was able to understand them in the 21st century, especially in light of current challenges we face today, challenges which are rooted in our history.

The result of this searching and research is this chapbook, which contains poems about my kin, their imagined lives based on what historical and anecdotal information acquired during my research. Some poems are set in more recent times but reflect my ongoing desire for peace and understanding in the world.

Notes

"William Joseph Owen": all historical information appeared in ancestry.com.

"Charley A. Owen": Looney's Tavern in Winston County, Alabama, was the meeting place where pro-Union men met and refused to secede from the Union. Many of the Winston men joined Union forces. Many who refused the oath of loyal to the Confederacy

were shot. Because Charley and his brother stole horses and cattle from the Union, they were arrested by the Union, then released. When Charley returned to a Winston County which would not let him vote. However, in 1877, ten years after this depiction, Cullman County was formed out of parts of Morgan, Winston, and Blount Counties. Charley did not have to move and lived the rest of his life in the same place.

"Minzie Mary Russell Talks on the 11th Regiment, Tennessee Cavalry": Minzie (Mary) Russell's son, Calvin died on March 24. Calvin was 19. His death is also depicted in "Vigil Strange." She died on August 29, 1863. Archibald Russell, Minzie's husband, remarried and had one daughter, Susan, with his second wife, Cynthia.

"Vigil Strange": Bloodgood was Union Lt. Col. at Brentwood TN. He had to surrender after Gen. Forrest, commanding the 2nd brigade. Referring to Primitive Baptists worship practices, church members sing only a cap pela and read from the Bible, hence the label "primitive." The U. S. Census of 1850 and 1860 listed no slaves in the Archibald Russell home. In 1870, there was one white child listed, and in 1890, two white servants.

"Nannie B Russell" and *"Mary Russell Humphrey"*: These poems are derived from the story of Nannie B Russell's death in childbirth on July 12, 1905. Her daughter, Nannie B Chandler, was taken to live with her aunt Mary Russell Humphrey for three years. Mary died in 1910, less than two years after giving up her niece. The details are depicted in *Searching for Nannie B: Connecting Three Generations of Southern Women* (Ardent Writer Press, 2015).

"Stayin' On": The information on George Sanders is from a story a 1937 interview by Preston, Klein, Federal Writers' Project. It was republished on the web site Alabama Pioneers, on July 24, 2017.

Martin Luther King's speech, "The Other American," was delivered at Grosse Point High School on March 14, 1968. Bernadette Athuahene's story in the *New York Times,* July 22, 2017, "Don't Let Detroit's Revival Rest on an Injustice," provided the quotes from Mr. Jones.

Acknowledgments

Poems previously published are as follows:

The Dead Mule School of Southern Literature (December 2107): "Minzie Mary Russell Talks on the 11th Regiment, Tennessee Cavalry," Vigil Strange," "Ghosts: Francis Marion Chandler"
Searching for Nannie B: Connecting Three Generations of Southern Women (Ardent Writers Press, 2015): "A Family Name"

Over many years, I have had the support of poet friends who have given me prompts, written with me, read my work and commented on my poems. Rick Bailey and Olga Klekner inspired me to write in the years before we moved from Michigan to Arizona. I thank Alexander Morgan for sharing his experience as a southerner and listening to mine. Russ Thorburn, fine poet and editor, has helped to arrange these poems as well as urged me to "go to the well" again and again to find stories in my ancestors. Thanks to Carole Kane, new-found Owen cousin, who has provided me with photos and family lore. I am honored by and thankful to FutureCycle Press and editor Diane Kistner for doing good work in the world and for believing in mine.

Thanks to my husband Roger Zeigler and my late sister Betty Emery for listening to first drafts and letting me know what works. To other friends who have listened to and read poems, Danny Rebb and Sally Borden, I thank you for honoring me with your attention and time. To Wallace McCord, who helped me remember my "southern" self.

My mother, Nannie B. Chandler Nelson, never stopped thinking about poetry. I thank her for the reminder of its importance in the world.

About FutureCycle Press

FutureCycle Press is dedicated to publishing lasting English-language poetry books, chapbooks, and anthologies in both print-on-demand and Kindle ebook formats. Founded in 2007 by long-time independent editor/publishers and partners Diane Kistner and Robert S. King, the press incorporated as a nonprofit in 2012. A number of our editors are distinguished poets and writers in their own right, and we have been actively involved in the small press movement going back to the early seventies.

The FutureCycle Poetry Book Prize and honorarium is awarded annually for the best full-length volume of poetry we publish in a calendar year. Introduced in 2013, our Good Works projects are anthologies devoted to issues of universal significance, with all proceeds donated to a related worthy cause. Our Selected Poems series highlights contemporary poets with a substantial body of work to their credit; with this series we strive to resurrect work that has had limited distribution and is now out of print.

We are dedicated to giving all of the authors we publish the care their work deserves, making our catalog of titles the most diverse and distinguished it can be, and paying forward any earnings to fund more great books.

We've learned a few things about independent publishing over the years. We've also evolved a unique, resilient publishing model that allows us to focus mainly on vetting and preserving for posterity poetry collections of exceptional quality without becoming overwhelmed with bookkeeping and mailing, fundraising activities, or taxing editorial and production "bubbles." To learn more about what we are doing, come see us at www.futurecycle.org.

www.ingramcontent.com/pod-product-compliance
Lightning Source LLC
Chambersburg PA
CBHW060046050426
42448CB00012B/3133